000601827

TALENT

Jackson County Library System
Medford, OR 97501

DATE DUE			
MAY 25 '95			
JUL 21 '95			
SEP 15 '95			
9-29			
NOV 22 '95			
FEB 16 '99			
MAY 11 '99			
DEC 18 '00			
MAY 8 '01			
JUL 9 '01			
MAY 07 '02			
OCT 22 '02			

T2-CBB-771

APR 5 - 1995

Jackson

County

Library

System

HEADQUARTERS:

413 W. Main

Medford, Oregon   97501

GAYLORD M2G

THE JUNIOR LIBRARY OF
AMERICAN INDIANS

THE
NEZ PERCE
INDIANS

Mark Rifkin

CHELSEA HOUSE PUBLISHERS
New York Philadelphia

JACKSON COUNTY LIBRARY SYSTEM
MEDFORD, OREGON 97501

The Nez Perces were the first tribe to breed horses, making the animals faster and stronger. Horses enabled the Nez Perces to travel longer distances for trade with other tribes or with the non-Indians who came to the West in the 1800s.

CHAPTER 1

Fox and Coyote

A long, long time ago, at the beginning of the world, there were no people. The Earth was ruled by animals—and monsters. In the Clearwater River country in the northwestern United States, in the heart of the Rocky Mountains, one of the most horrible monsters who ever lived roamed freely. The animals named him the Kamiah Monster, for two reasons. The first was because he lived in the Kamiah Valley, and the second was because he was as big as the whole Kamiah Valley itself.

This huge, ugly Kamiah Monster stomped through the land, eating every animal he saw. In a single swallow he devoured the largest of animals, and every time he ate he

According to legend, this hill is the heart of the Kamiah Monster, from which the Nez Perces were created. It is located near present-day Kamiah, Idaho.

so many of the animals and there were no people. Coyote understood the problem, but he did not know what he could do about it. All the pieces of the monster had been used to make tribes. There was nothing left of the giant except a few drops of the blood of the monster's heart that were still on Coyote's fingers. Suddenly, Coyote had an idea.

Coyote scattered the drops of the Kamiah Monster's blood over the land. These few drops became the last of all the Indian tribes, the Nez Perces. Nez Perce was a name later given to these people by the French explorers of their land; they called themselves the Nimapu (NEE-MA-POO), which means the Real People. They called themselves the Nimapu because they came from the blood of the monster's heart, not his body, and so had been born of strength, courage, and honor.

For those who were afraid that the Nimapu would be evil because they came from the monster's heart, there was little need to fear. The first thing Coyote had done was cut out the monster's evil heart and leave it to rot away along with the monster's liver. Today the heart and the liver of the terrible creature can still be seen, transformed over the centuries into two mounds of rock across the Clearwater River from the Kamiah Valley.

Silver medals like this, showing a white hand shaking an Indian hand, were given by the Corps of Discovery to Indian leaders during the Lewis and Clark expedition as a symbol of friendship.

CHAPTER 2

The Real People

The Real People lived in communities in the present-day states of northern Idaho, southeastern Washington, and northeastern Oregon, along the Snake, Salmon, and Clearwater rivers. They settled near the mouths of small streams and riverbanks because the fishing was good there.

Their permanent dwellings were structures known as *longhouses*, in which as many as 30 families would live together. One or two of these longhouses would make up a village. On cold winter nights the children would gather around the village elders in the longhouses and listen to stories about the people's history, religion, and tradition. The

Mexico. Over time, through trade, warfare, and theft, Indian tribes across the continent began to acquire horses of their own. Horses made a huge difference in the way of life of the Nez Perces and other tribes. Suddenly, they could travel farther when hunting or gathering, and they could move quicker when at war. The Nez Perces were the first tribe to actually breed horses, making the animals stronger, faster, and more useful for specific tasks. As they traveled greater dis-

A Nez Perce camp on the Yellowstone River in what today is Montana, photographed by William Henry Jackson in 1871.

tances and met more tribes, the Nez Perces began to hear stories about the white man.

On September 20, 1805, the explorer William Clark and six hunters, after splitting off from their main group, were traveling through a wide, open land in present-day Idaho, known today as the Weippe Prairie, when they saw three young Indian boys. The boys quickly ran away and hid from the men. They had heard stories about white men, but they had never before seen one. They were afraid that the white men might hurt them.

But Clark did not want to hurt them. He was on a mission to explore land, west of the Mississippi River, that the United States had acquired the year before through the Louisiana Purchase. He and Meriwether Lewis had been asked by President Thomas Jefferson to take a party of men, known as the *Corps of Discovery*, through this territory and gather information about the land and the people that they saw.

Not wanting to scare the Indian boys, Clark took off his gun and then looked for the boys in the tall grass. He found two of them, offered them small gifts, and explained in sign language that he had come in peace. Clark and his men were soon led to the village of Broken Arm, a great war chief. At the time, Broken Arm was away with most of the men

they wished to reach the Pacific Ocean by wintertime, the Nez Perces drew them maps and helped them build canoes from the many tall cedar trees that grew in the region.

When the white men had to leave, Twisted Hair and other Nez Perces came along and helped guide them through the dangerous waters that led to the ocean. When one of the canoes split open, the Indians helped rescue the white men and their equipment. In return for their kindness, the Indians were given many gifts, including cloth, flags, ribbons, and medals made of silver. The medals had the words *Peace and Friendship* on them as well as an engraving of a white hand shaking an Indian hand. These medals became treasured by the Indians.

The Corps of Discovery continued its travels and soon came once again upon the village of Broken Arm. The Nez Perces explained to the white men that they wanted peace among all the warring Indian tribes so that they would be able to trade safely with the white man in trading posts. The white men said that they would try to establish peace in the territory, and a feast was held. When the Corps eventually had to leave, Lewis wrote in his diary that "the [white men] . . . would [always] give them every assistance in their power; that [the Indians] were poor but their hearts were good."

The Nez Perces and the men of the Lewis and Clark expedition had become trusting friends. The white men gave the Indians gifts and much medical assistance. The Indians gave the white men food and shelter and helped them travel down the rivers and through the prairie. The white men thought of the Nez Perces as an honorable, friendly, and very proud people. The Indians looked forward to seeing the white men again and to obtaining more goods from them. Little did they know that Lewis had also written in his diary that "this country would form an extensive settlement." Lewis and Clark and the rest of the Corps of Discovery may have been grateful to the Indians and enjoyed meeting them, but other whites could not wait to take the sacred land away from the Real People. ▲

Though they wanted the guns and metal goods the traders brought, the Nez Perce were not especially interested in hunting beavers. They regarded the work as demeaning and drudgery, and they told one trader that they were insulted the whites wanted them to "crawl about searching for furs."

Soon, there were charges of stealing and cheating and incidents of fighting between the whites and the Indians. One of the leading traders, Donald McKenzie, shot several Nez Perce horses and threatened to shoot many more unless they agreed to sell him some. Another trader, John Clarke, hanged a Palouse Indian in public for stealing goods. The Palouse Indian had many friends among the Nez Perces. By 1818, the friendly relationship between the whites and the Nez Perces seemed doomed.

That year, McKenzie helped build Fort Nez Perces, which he named in honor of the great tribe in an attempt to rebuild good relations with the Indians. But the North West Company found out later that the post, which was on the east bank of the Columbia River in the present-day state of Washington, had in fact been built outside of Nez Perce territory. In 1825, after the North West Company merged with the Hudson's Bay Company, the post was renamed Fort Walla Walla.

The arrival of the white man had an enormous effect on the Indians' life. But it was two things that the white man brought with him—his religion and his medicine—that changed the course of Nez Perce history forever.

A brass powder flask, glass beads, a fire striker, and a dagger—items which the Nez Perces obtained through trade with non-Indians.

Isaac Ingalls Stevens was appointed governor of Washington Territory in 1853. He negotiated treaties that robbed Indians of their rights.

Indians had no natural immunity. In 1846 and 1847, smallpox and measles killed hundreds of Indians, who were growing less and less friendly with the whites.

On November 29, 1847, Marcus and Narcissa Whitman, along with twelve others, were massacred at Waiilatpu by the Cayuses. At about the same time, the Nez Perces attacked Spalding's mission. Though they did not succeed in driving the missionary away permanently, they did inspire the whites in the region to raise an army to fight them. Meanwhile, an increasing number of white settlers continued to move into the Nez Perces' territory.

In 1853 the Nez Perce homeland, and that of a number of other Pacific Northwest tribes, was turned into the Washington Territory, and President Franklin Pierce appointed Isaac Ingalls Stevens governor there. The Nez Perces had lost control of their own land. They had heard about the *removal policy* of the U.S. government from eastern Indians: the government would place agents in charge of the Indians, who would be removed from their homelands, or relocated, to *reservation* lands, which were overseen by the *Bureau of Indian Affairs*. But the Nez Perces never thought it would happen to them. ▲

The arrival of the Nez Perce Indians at the Walla Walla treaty grounds in May 1855.

CHAPTER 4

The Walla Walla Council

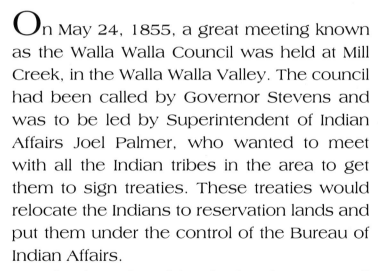

On May 24, 1855, a great meeting known as the Walla Walla Council was held at Mill Creek, in the Walla Walla Valley. The council had been called by Governor Stevens and was to be led by Superintendent of Indian Affairs Joel Palmer, who wanted to meet with all the Indian tribes in the area to get them to sign treaties. These treaties would relocate the Indians to reservation lands and put them under the control of the Bureau of Indian Affairs.

At the time, the whites had no interest at all in the reservation lands, but they wanted the Indians' home territory in order to build a railroad across it. The bureau planned to train the Indians to live more like whites; they wanted to destroy the Indians' traditional culture. Expecting trouble, the whites brought 47 gunmen with them to the Walla Walla Council, but it would not be enough to prevent trouble.

More than 1,000 Nez Perces arrived at the meeting. According to the son of Governor Stevens, they arrived with "their faces covered with white, red, and yellow paint in fanciful designs, and decked with plumes and feathers and trinkets fluttering in the sunshine," exhibiting their horsemanship, beating drums, whooping, and singing. More than 4,000 other Indians also came, not in such grand splendor but equally determined to show Stevens and his people their dedication to their traditional ways and to demonstrate that they were not prepared to give in to their demands.

Most of the Nez Perces were not prowhite or pro-Christian. They did not want their children to become "farmers and mechanics . . . doctors and lawyers like white men," as Stevens said they would. They did not want to lose their heritage or their land—the very land from which they were born. Stevens said that "you have to have your tract; the rest to be the Great Father's (President Franklin Pierce) for his white children." The Indians saw through the words of

Lawyer, a Nez Perce chief who possibly struck a deal with the governor in which the Nez Perces would move to a reservation and not oppose the government.

Stevens and Palmer and the rest of the whites, who had underestimated the intelligence of the Indians. The Cayuse leader Yellow Bird warned Stevens and Palmer to "speak straight. . . . You have spoken in a manner partly tending to evil. Speak plain to us. . . ." But the tribes soon realized that if they did not agree to the treaty, they would have no land at all.

Most historians agree that there was nothing the Nez Perces could have done to save their interests. It is very possible that Lawyer, one of the many Nez Perce chiefs there, had already struck a deal with Stevens in which the Nez Perces would peacefully move to a reservation and would not oppose the government; they would be "civilized." Lawyer told his people that he trusted Stevens and that the Nez Perces' "old laws are poor, the new laws we are getting are good laws, and are straight." He even referred to the white men as "brothers."

In the end, the Nez Perces signed the treaty, as did the Palouses, the Yakimas, the Umatillas, the Cayuses, the Walla Wallas, and the Columbia River tribes. But nobody was happy. When the great Nez Perce leader Looking Glass arrived after the council had ended, he cried out, "My People, what have

Chief Timothy, a Nez Perce leader who helped Colonel Edward Steptoe in his battle with the Palouses. Timothy was prowhite, pro-Christian, and protreaty.

you done? While I was gone, you have sold my country." The opposition to the original agreements led to three more treaties, signed in June 1855, which created the Nez Perce, Yakima, and Umatilla reservations. Looking Glass was still not happy with the land given the Nez Perces, but Stevens had in effect taken his power away and bestowed it upon the prowhite Lawyer. (The treaty went so far as to promise to Lawyer a personal payment of $500 a year for 20 years, his own house, and his own 10 acres of land that would be plowed and fenced at government expense.) The Indians were promised that these treaties would not go into effect for two or three years, but within months white gold prospectors were flooding into the Washington Territory, and the Plateau Indian War of 1855–58 had begun.

The Plateau Indian War involved the Cayuses, the Yakimas, the Walla Wallas, and the Umatillas; the Nez Perces, for the most part, remained neutral and stayed out of the fighting. Two exceptions were Captain John, a Nez Perce scout who served with Colonel Benjamin Franklin Shaw, and Chief Timothy, a progressive Nez Perce leader who, along with his brother Levi and 13 others, helped Colonel Edward Steptoe in his battle with the Palouses.

Timothy was engaged in a bitter dispute with the Palouse chief Tilcoax. Timothy was prowhite, pro-Christian, and protreaty, and he favored teaching his people English and the ways of the white man. Tilcoax believed strongly in the traditional ways and was against white intervention. Although he probably signed the Yakima Treaty, Tilcoax quickly withdrew his consent and joined a war party dedicated to opposing the whites.

Timothy believed that by helping Steptoe he could use the white soldiers to get to his enemy, but neither Timothy nor Steptoe were prepared for what they saw when they met the Palouses near the present-day border of Washington and Idaho. Steptoe had thought that defeating the Indians would be easy, so he brought few men and very little ammunition. But the Indians were ready for him; Steptoe suddenly found himself surrounded by "ten or twelve hundred Indians of various tribes—Spokanes, Palouses, Coeur d'Alenes, Yakimas, and some others—all armed, painted, and defiant," in the words of one of the soldiers present. The Indians did

Nez Perce warriors ready to defend their territory.

not attack but sat on their colorfully painted horses, simply watching the soldiers, tormenting them.

The Coeur d'Alene chief, Vincent, then met with Steptoe to talk. Levi grew impatient and soon joined them. He took out his riding whip and struck Vincent, saying, "Proud man, why do you not fire?" He was taunting his own people. He had whipped an Indian on his own to defend the white man. Vincent told him that "hereafter you will be ashamed of having struck" another Indian and rode off. After some fighting among the Indians themselves, a battle ensued in which the Indian force easily chased the soldiers away. The Indians could have massacred the white army; however, they chose not to. They had won, and they had made the point that they would defend their territory with their lives.

But the fighting was far from over. The Nez Perces as a people may not have been involved in the Plateau Indian War, but they were soon to find themselves in the center of the battle that would decide the entire fate of their nation—the Nez Perce War of 1877. ▲

Chief Joseph, a Nez Perce leader who refused to give up Indian land to the U.S. government.

CHAPTER 5

"We Will Not Sell the Land"

The discovery of gold in the Pacific Northwest brought thousands of prospectors to the Nez Perce reservation. Although legally they were not allowed to dig for gold there, they came with their equipment and even set up little tent cities filled with gamblers, whiskey peddlers, and merchants. The introduction of whiskey to the reservation was especially troublesome. By 1861, drunkenness was common on the reservation, and many drunken Indians were robbed and killed by whites.

The whites soon sought to negotiate a new treaty with the Nez Perces, one that would decrease their property to allow the prospectors to dig where they wanted to. Accordingly, the Lapwai Council began on May 25, 1863. Although some of the more powerful chiefs were not yet present at the council, all the other chiefs, including the prowhite Lawyer, were outraged that the whites would go back on their word. The chiefs staunchly refused to renegotiate. Lawyer read aloud

This 1868 photograph of Nez Perce chiefs Timothy, Lawyer, and Jason (seated, left to right), and four white men was probably taken after an amendment to the 1863 treaty was negotiated.

the words of Governor Stevens himself, who had said, "My friends, we have assembled under the influence of Laws, and that which shall be permanent and straight." Lawyer, who had been so instrumental in giving the government all that it had wanted eight years earlier, now argued, "You but trifle with us. We cannot give you the country, we cannot sell it to you."

After a six-day break, the council reopened, but this time with all the chiefs, including Old Joseph, Eagle From The Light, and Big Thunder, present and ready to fight for their land. They offered to sell a small amount of Nez Perce land, mostly that which held the gold, but the government officials wanted more. They met individually with each of the chiefs, and soon some of them, including Lawyer and Timothy, were willing to sell land to the whites so long as the Nez Perces retained most of the reservation.

The other leaders vehemently refused to listen to the whites and grew very angry with those leaders who were succumbing to the whites' wishes. Agent Charles Hutchins told the antitreaty chiefs that "the good Nez Perces will be wise, and rich and happy. You will be poor and miserable. . . . If you persist in your disloyalty, we shall not regard you as Nez Perces."

Ultimately, government officials ignored Old Joseph, Eagle From The Light, and Big Thunder and instead signed a new treaty with Lawyer and 51 of his followers; not a single antitreaty leader signed. The Nez Perce Treaty of 1863 gave nearly 7 million acres—almost 90 percent of the remaining Nez Perce land—to the whites for a mere

General Oliver O. Howard was known as the "Christian General." An opponent of the Washani faith of the Nez Perces, he represented the U.S. government at the Second Lapwai Council.

eight cents an acre. (But, as was true of the 1855 treaty, actual payment was scarce.)

The old Nez Perce leadership was angry. Their land had been sold right out from under them by a small group of their own people. They called the agreement the Thief Treaty; they felt that they had been robbed. Many of the Indians refused to obey the new treaty. Years later, referring to the ceded land, Chief Young Joseph claimed that "we never sold it." In the early 1870s, two agents wrote to the commissioner of Indian Affairs that "the treaty of 1863 is not binding upon Joseph and his band," and that the government should give the land back to the Nez Perces and pay for the whites to leave. In August 1871, Old Joseph, on his deathbed, told his son, Young Joseph, "Always remember that your father never sold his country. You must stop your ears whenever you are asked to sign a treaty selling your home."

The government appeared to agree, and President Ulysses S. Grant, on June 16, 1873, conceded the Indians control of the land in the Wallowa Valley. Unfortunately, an error made by an official in Washington, D.C., gave the Indians the wrong part of the valley (the prairie, where the whites lived, instead of the lake and the upper part of the river), and problems between the whites and the Indians only grew. The whites would not leave any part of the valley until they received payment from the government, so the two factions were in constant conflict.

A Modoc rebellion that year furthered the whites' belief that *all* Indians in the Northwest should be moved to reservations. Also, the government was becoming fearful of the increasing power of the Indians' holy people, who were stressing more than ever that Indians reject white ways and religion and instead fight for their traditions and their homeland. But then Agent John Monteith, a former supporter of Young Joseph's, turned against the spread of this faith, the Washani, and told the Nez Perces that they

Two Moons (far right), the principal tooat (medicine person), performing a dance at Nespelem.

must move onto the small reservation that had been set aside for them. On June 10, 1875, President Grant cancelled his previous order in favor of the continued removal of nontreaty Indians.

Many of the whites who lived in the Wallowa Valley actually were upset with the reversal. They were prepared to leave the land for the Indians, but only if they were to be paid by the government as had been outlined in the first order. Now there was no more incentive for them to leave the valley.

During this time, General Oliver O. Howard met with Joseph. He agreed with Joseph that the Indians should not be forced to leave the Wallowa Valley. He knew that the white settlers there were willing to leave in return for government compensation, and he believed strongly that the treaty of 1863 was indeed a Thief Treaty.

Following the questionable killing at the hands of whites of a well-respected Indian named Wilhautyah, who was a close friend of Joseph's, General Howard sent Major Henry Clay Wood to investigate further the situation of the Nez Perces at Wallowa. Major Wood reported that "the non-treaty Nez Perces cannot in law be regarded as bound by the treaty of 1863." Wood said that in order to preserve peace, the Indians should let the white courts decide the fate of the two men responsible for the death of Wilhautyah. (Neither one was ever convicted of the murder.) Howard and Joseph also wanted to call a new council to restore the complete Nez Perce homeland.

The new Lapwai Council began on November 13, 1876. One major difference between this council and the previous ones was that Lawyer was not present. He had died on January 3. Since his death, the strength of the nontreaty bands who lived off the reservation and refused to obey the laws of the white man had grown dramatically. Thus, no major prowhite Indians attended the council with Joseph and his band.

The officials immediately told Joseph that he must leave the Wallowa Valley and move onto the Nez Perce reservation as agreed to in the 1863 treaty. Joseph responded by proclaiming his pride in and dedication to the land and his religion, which preached the sanctity of the earth. Joseph's proclamation of faith in the Washani religion alienated Howard, who was known as the Christian General. Howard compared the spiritual leaders of the Washani faith with devils and witches and suddenly challenged Joseph. Though only a year earlier Howard had

continued on page 57

PLATEAU FINERY

In the early 1800s, the whites who came to the Nez Perce territory introduced the Indians to many new objects. Some of the items the Indians obtained in trade were glass beads and woolen cloth. The Nez Perces used these new items to make and decorate their horse gear, ceremonial objects, and clothing.

The Nez Perces received the products from non-Indians, but they copied the beadwork designs and horse gear from other tribes, such as the Cheyenne and the Crow Indians. The Crows often offered to trade their bead-work for the Nez Perces' horses. Finally, the Nez Perces learned to make designs like the Crows'.

The Indians of the Northeast and the Great Lakes, who imitated beaded floral patterns from the Europeans, brought new designs to the attention of the Nez Perces. The Nez Perces quickly mastered these creative patterns and soon developed their own characteristic designs. The colors the Nez Perces chose were brighter than the dark shades preferred by the Eastern Indians, and the objects the Nez Perces decorated were among the most colorful produced by any Indian tribe.

Beaded ornaments such as this were placed on the foreheads of the Nez Perce's horses during special social and ceremonial occasions.

A martingale, or horse collar, made from red woolen cloth and adorned with glass beads, brass bells, and dyed horsehair tassels.

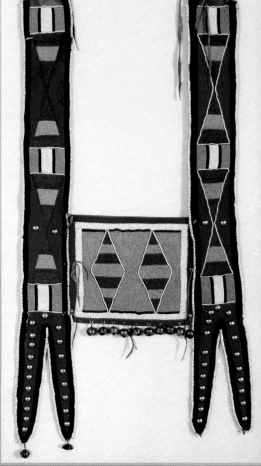

The outlining of shapes and the use of isosceles triangles in the pattern on this martingale are characteristic of the work of Crow artists.

A woman's saddle carved from green cottonwood. Excellent examples of Nez Perce beadwork are found on the pommels and stirrup.

The red cloth of this martingale came from a Hudson's Bay Company blanket. Other materials used include brass sequins, purple and blue felt, and blue and red beads.

A headdress constructed from wool cloth and rawhide, decorated with glass beads, and topped with deer antlers. It was worn by a medicine man during ceremonies and hunting expeditions.

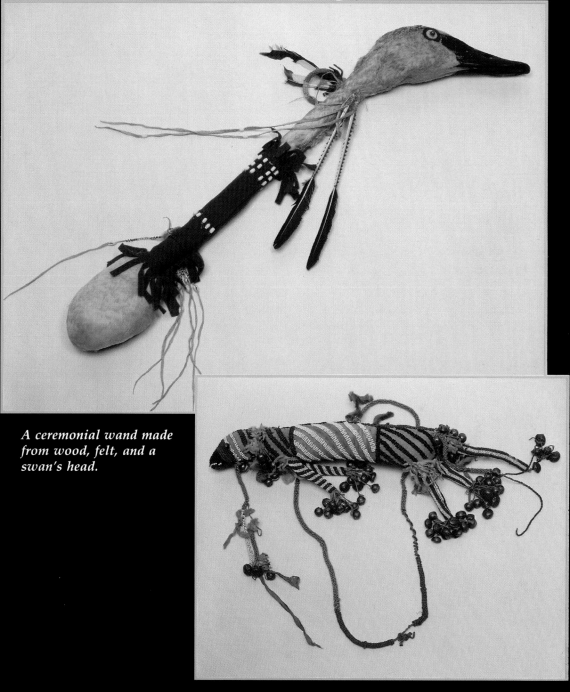

A ceremonial wand made from wood, felt, and a swan's head.

A beaded otter effigy that was used in healing ceremonies. Brass bells are attached to its neck, feet, and tail.

A pair of leather gloves adorned with fringe. The intricate floral patterns show the influence of Great Lakes Indian beadwork on Nez Perce artisans.

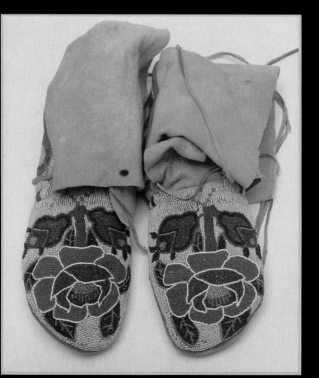

A single red flower decorates the toe of each of these beaded moccasins.

*The red, white, and blue beads on this pair of moccasins
create a geometric design reminiscent of those used by
Indian artists of the Plains.*

The glass beads on this early-19th-century elk hide dress were made in Italy, China, and the Netherlands, evidence of the wealth of foreign goods then available to the Nez Perce through their dealings with non-Indian traders.

continued from page 48

referred to the Indians as "proud-spirited, self-supporting, and intelligent," he now mistakenly believed that Joseph and his band had come under the influence of Smohalla, leader of the *tooats*, or dreamers, as the medicine people of the Washani faith were known. The tooats taught that the Nez Perces should reject white religion, white rule, and the reservations.

Joseph refused to give up the Nez Perce land. "We will not sell the land," Joseph said. "We will not give up the land. We love the land; it is our home." The government officials left Lapwai with nothing having been resolved except their total disregard for the tooats, who were firmly opposed to the authority of the United States.

The government was now being urged to forcibly relocate the nontreaty Indians onto the reservation land. Four of the five officials present at the Lapwai Council recommended that force be used. Only Major Wood believed that force was not necessary and should not be used. When the nontreaty Nez Perces and Palouses heard of this, they called for another meeting—the Second Lapwai Council, held in 1877.

At the Second Lapwai Council, Howard and Monteith represented the government, and Toohoolhoolzote and Husishusis

Kute were chosen to speak for the Indians. Toohoolhoolzote's defense of his religion and claims of "chieftainship of the earth" angered Howard, who shouted back that the Indians had signed a treaty in 1863 and that they must obey it. The two argued continually until Howard lost his temper and had the Indian leader arrested and imprisoned in front of all the Indians at Fort Lapwai.

The other Indians now believed that their only defense was war, but influenced by the heartfelt words of Ollokot, Joseph's younger brother, who urged them not to break the peace, they decided to give in to the general's demands. They were given little more than a month to say good-bye to their homeland. Many of them wept as they left

The Camas Prairie. Before the Nez Perces moved to the reservation in 1877, they held one last harvest celebration there.

behind their sacred land and the special spiritual relationship that they had shared with the earth since the very beginning of their people. They held one last harvest celebration on the Camas Prairie, and then they were no longer free. ▲

Young Looking Glass, who with his people was drawn into the Nez Perce War of 1877 with General Howard's attack on their village.

CHAPTER **6**

"It Was a Bloody Battle"

While camped at Camas Prairie, a young man named Wahlitits was convinced by other Nez Perces to avenge the death of his father, Eagle Robe, who had been murdered the year before by a white settler named Larry Ott. From his deathbed, Eagle Robe had asked his son not to seek revenge. Wahlitits had tried to obey his father's dying wishes, but too much had happened to him and his people for him to remain quiet any longer.

With two of his friends, Swan Necklace and Red Moccasin Tops, Wahlitits began raiding white settlements, searching for Ott. Although they could not find Ott, they did find other whites who had harassed their people. They killed three men and wounded another. In order to preserve peace, Nez Perce chief White Bird formed a war party to try to stop Wahlitits's rampage. But nothing could prevent the young warrior from seeking revenge.

The Nez Perces who were camped at Camas Prairie soon learned of Wahlitits's actions. They decided to move south to White Bird Canyon, where they could meet the white troops and try to prevent any further fighting. But they would be prepared to defend themselves if there was no other way.

Soon Captain David Perry, the man who had been put in charge of the arrest of Toohoolhoolzote, arrived in White Bird Canyon with a force that included whites and protreaty Nez Perces. Indian fought Indian. The Nez Perces successfully drove Perry and his men away, but the Indians were confused. They had wanted to avoid war at all costs, but now it seemed that they were being thrust into a war that they did not want to fight.

At Weippe Prairie, the Nez Perces met to decide what to do next. Led by the insistence of Young Looking Glass, they retreated over the Bitterroot Mountains and into the Bitterroot Valley in Montana. It would have been easy for the Nez Perces at this point to leave the United States and move into Canada, avoiding any further conflict with the U.S. Army. But they did not believe that the army wanted them dead; they thought that the government merely wanted their land. The Nez Perces were a humane people who had lived together with the white man in the past. They did not understand violence. They had been raised to respect one another and to love the land. They did not want to fight the white man. So they gave the land to them. But at the Big Hole, a valley in Montana, the Nez Perces found out that the U.S.

View of the battleground of the Big Hole. The Nez Perces camped at this site to rest after two months of travel and were unprepared for an attack by the U.S. Army.

government wanted much more than just their territory.

On August 9, 1877, an army led by Colonel John Gibbon sneaked up on the Nez Perce camp and showered the people with bullets. There was little the Nez Perces could do to defend themselves. Gibbon had instructed his men to take no prisoners. One Nez Perce, Wounded Head, said, "It was a bloody battle." In the end, between 60 and 90 Nez Perces were killed—mostly women and children. The Nez Perce women had been extremely brave. During the long and difficult journey to the Big Hole, the women had cared for the children, nursed the sick and the wounded, and had even served as warriors. About the battle, Joseph said, "The Nez Perce never make war on women and children . . . we would feel ashamed to do so." In fact, Joseph felt ashamed to kill anyone, but the actions of the white man had propelled him and his people into a war they never wanted.

The Nez Perces, now under the leadership of Lean Elk (the people had lost faith in Looking Glass because he had led them into the Big Hole, assuring them they would be safe there), began to move north. After the Crows refused to help them, they had no choice but to follow the lead of Sitting Bull and other Sioux and head into Canada. They knew they

Colonel Nelson A. Miles of the U.S. Army persuaded most of the Nez Perces to surrender and retreat to the reservation in October 1877.

were being followed by General Howard, but they did not know that Colonel Nelson A. Miles had been sent to cut them off before they could make it to Canada. Looking Glass, arguing that the people and the horses were too tired to continue on at the present pace, wrested control of the tribe away from Lean Elk and convinced the people that they must slow down. And so the Nez Perces took a fateful rest at Snake Creek, between the Little Rocky Mountains and Bear Paw Mountains—only 40 miles and less than two days away from freedom.

Miles, aided by Cheyenne and Sioux scouts, came upon the Nez Perce camp and attacked. A bloody battle ensued in which even women and children, using digging sticks and butcher knives, engaged in hand-to-hand combat with the soldiers. Some of the bravest and wisest Nez Perces were killed in this battle, including Ollokot, Too-hoolhoolzote, and Lean Elk. But after losing too many of his men, Miles ordered a retreat. On October 1, 1877, Miles called a truce in order to talk with Joseph about the terms of the Indians' surrender.

Miles wanted the Indians to lay down all of their arms, but Joseph wanted the Nez Perces to be able to keep half for hunting. The two leaders could not reach an agreement.

After Miles said, "If you will come and give up your arms, I will spare your lives and send you back to the reservation," more than 400 of the Nez Perces remained with Joseph and surrendered. Some escaped to Canada but did not find even there the freedom and peace they sought. Refusing to surrender, Looking Glass decided to join those who were bound for Canada; but before he could leave he was shot in the head. He was the last Nez Perce killed in the great war. Years later, Ollokot's wife, one of those who made it to Canada, said about the war, "Strong men, well women, and little children killed and buried. They had not done wrong to be so killed. We had only asked to be left in our homes. . . . But we would be free. . . ." They would not be free for long.

Despite Miles's promise that the Nez Perces would be returned to their reservation in Idaho, the Indians soon found themselves imprisoned at Fort Leavenworth, Kansas. The Nez Perces were treated horribly there, and they suffered from malnutrition, malaria, and other diseases. Many of them died.

In July 1878, the Nez Perces were moved to the Quapaw Agency in Indian Territory. A year later they were moved to the Ponca Agency in what is now Tonkawa, Oklahoma. The U.S. government had not prepared the

With Chief Joseph, Yellow Bull (pictured) traveled to Washington, D.C., to speak with federal officials about the Nez Perces returning to their land.

agency for the arrival of the Nez Perces, so there was no food, clothing, or medicine for them. Still more died. The Nez Perces hated Indian Territory. They called it Eekish Pah— the Hot Place.

But they were not ready to give in completely. Husishusis Kute led the people in Washani prayers, as the Nez Perces tried to hold on to their traditions and pray for deliverance even though they had lost everything. Joseph, Husishusis Kute, and Yellow Bull continued to talk to government officials in order to regain their land. Joseph was particularly forceful, going to Washington, D.C., and proclaiming the great history of the Nez Perces and their land and arguing for its return to them. He said, "The earth is the mother of all people, and all people should have equal rights upon it." He eloquently argued that the Nez Perces had been treated unfairly and that they should not have been exiled. But not until April 1885 was anything done.

Finally, the Nez Perces were allowed to return to their homeland. However, there was one catch: Joseph was among 150 Indians who were made to settle on the Colville Indian Reservation in Washington and could not join Husishusis Kute's group of 118 on their homeland. Those that returned to the

Nez Perce reservation found that much of their sacred land was not part of the reservation anymore, and they had to find new homes in their own land. Approximately 750 Nez Perces left the Camas Prairie, searching for a new home. In November 1877, 418 Nez Perces were sent to Leavenworth. Less than eight years later, only 268 made it to the Colville and Nez Perce reservations.

A once-proud, earth-loving, and peaceful people had been all but destroyed by the U.S. government. During the war, General Howard's lack of success against the Nez Perces had made him a laughingstock. Much of the American public admired and respected the Nez Perces; many even rooted for their ultimate victory. The Nez Perces had fought valiantly. They became recognized for their great strength and courage, yet lost because they were severely outnumbered. The United States spent almost $2 million and lost many men fighting the Nez Perces. But even in the end, after having taken the Indians' lives, homes, and possessions, after depriving them of their traditions, their history, and their land, there was one thing the white man could not take away from them: their pride. ▲

A Nez Perce man performing a hoop dance in Yakima, Washington, in 1987.

CHAPTER 7

Allotment and the Loss of the Land

From the end of the Nez Perce War to the present, much of the story of the Nez Perces has taken place in Congress. The first major development came in the 1880s when Senator Henry L. Dawes proposed that the reservations be divided into small tracts of land called *allotments*. These allotments would become the private property of individual Indians. According to some non-Indians, the Indians would take better care of the land because they owned it. These people, however, failed to realize that many

Indians are not farmers. Others who favored the allotments did so because they knew that the Indians were interested primarily in the land along the rivers, so the rest of the land would become available to non-Indians at a very cheap price.

As stated by the House Committee on Indian Affairs, "The real aim of this bill is to get the Indian lands and open them to settlement." In 1887, Congress passed the General Allotment Act, also known as the Dawes Act. Six years later, under the terms of the Nez Perce Allotment Agreement, the Nez Perces gave the United States 542,000 acres of unallotted land in return for $1,626,222 and the promise that the government would keep whites off the land until the Indians had their land titles. The Colville reservation was also allotted. Neither event proved to be a good thing for the Indians.

The government soon changed the laws to make it very easy for whites to buy land from the Indians. Unfortunately, the Indians did not quite understand the concept of selling land—they believed the earth was something that no human could own—and soon much of their land was lost. If not for the tribal elders, who refused to sell their land under any circumstances, even more of it would have been gone.

Allotment continued until 1934. By that time, the land owned by all the Indians had dropped from 3 billion acres in 1500 to 150 million acres in 1887 to a mere 48 million acres. In 1934, Congress passed the Indian Reorganization Act (IRA), which encouraged all Indians to preserve their cultural and historical heritage. But the act also established new guidelines for tribal governments, guidelines that were unacceptable to the Nez Perces. Some Nez Perces did not want to go back to the traditional ways, while others thought that accepting the IRA would increase government control of the tribe. Thus, the Nez Perce rejected the law, choosing not to become a tribe under the IRA. In 1948,

Nez Perce farmers on their allotment at Camp Corbett, Idaho, around the year 1900.

Nez Perce students at the Carlisle School in Pennsylvania.

however, the tribe worked with the government to restructure their constitution, which had been adopted in October 1927, and form the Nez Perce Tribal Executive Committee.

Much of the last hundred years for the Nez Perce has been spent in a tug-of-war between traditional ways and government control. Today many of the Nez Perces practice the Seven Drums Religion, a modern version of the Washani religion. These Indians continue the beliefs of their ancestors. They stress the traditions of the tribe while trying to keep the U.S. government out of their life. But another group of Nez Perces are striving for success in business while favoring modernization and government control.

Many Nez Perces today are college graduates. The tribe participates in such functions as the Trophy Pow Wow and Circle Celebration, competitions in which Indian men, women, and children vie for money, prizes, and trophies for their dancing, drumming, and singing. The Nez Perces still treasure their history, culture, and language. They continue to hold annual root ceremonies and war dance rituals, and in 1977 they celebrated the 100th anniversary of the Nez Perce War.

The Nez Perces enjoy sports as well. The men and women compete in basketball and softball leagues, and the children like to play volleyball, football, baseball, and other sports. Rodeos and fairs are also popular.

The Nez Perce Indians have had to struggle for survival ever since those three Nez Perce boys hid from William Clark in 1805. They have fought to protect their people, to keep their land, and to preserve their traditions. They have been cheated and lied to and taken advantage of. Yet they still believe in the strength of the spirit, and they will continue to maintain their culture. The Real People can not only look at their past with pride but can face the future with the knowledge that they will survive. ▲

CHRONOLOGY

Sept. 1805   The Corps of Discovery meet three Nez Perce boys, who eventually lead the white men to their village

1810s   Many trading posts are established in Nez Perce territory

1831   Four Nez Perces travel to St. Louis, Missouri, to find out more about Christianity

1836–47   Missionaries Henry and Eliza Spalding work closely with the Nez Perces to convert them to Christianity

1842   Dr. Elijah White establishes a set of laws that order the Indians receive physical and financial punishment for any wrongdoing

May 1855   The Walla Walla Council begins, leading to the signing of the Treaty of 1855

1855–58   The Plateau Indian War is fought

1863   The Nez Perce Treaty of 1863 cuts the size of the Nez Perce reservation by 90 percent

1876–77   Two Lapwai councils are held to try to settle land disputes

1877   The Nez Perce War leads to the imprisonment of the Nez Perces at Fort Leavenworth, Kansas

1887   The General Allotment Act divides up the reservations; the Nez Perces are split up between the Colville Indian Reservation in Washington and the Nez Perce reservation in Idaho

1893   The Nez Perce Allotment Agreement gives more Nez Perce land to the U.S. government

1934   The Nez Perces vote not to accept the terms of the Indian Reorganization Act

1977   The Nez Perces celebrate the 100th anniversary of the Nez Perce War by striking a silver medal with a likeness of Chief Joseph on it

GLOSSARY

agent   a U.S. government employee responsible for conducting official business with an Indian tribe

allotment   a U.S. government policy that divided Indian reservations into small, privately owned plots of land

Bureau of Indian Affairs   a U.S. government agency that managed trade with Indians; today it encourages Indians to control their own affairs

camas   a wild bulb that could be eaten; a staple food of the Nez Perce

Corps of Discovery   a party of men, headed by William Clark and Meriwether Lewis, who explored much of the territory west of the Mississippi River in order to gather information about the land and people

longhouse   a large, bark-covered dwelling that housed as many as 30 Nez Perce families

removal policy   the U.S. government policy that called for the relocation of Indians from their homelands to reservations

reservation   an area of land set aside by the U.S. government for Indian use

tooats   medicine people of the Washani faith; known as dreamers

wyakin   a guardian spirit power believed to watch over Indian children

Wyakwatset   a Nez Perce medicine ceremony in which individuals sang songs that they learned from their guardian spirits

INDEX

ABOUT THE AUTHOR

MARK RIFKIN is a Brooklyn-born writer and editor who has written often about Native Americans and the American West. His poetry has appeared in several children's books. Rifkin lives in Manhattan with his wife, Ellen, and their cat, Goat.

PICTURE CREDITS

Photograph by Jim Barker, courtesy of Laboratory of Anthropology, University of Idaho, p. 14; Photo by the Denver Public Library, Western History Department, p. 40; Idaho State Historical Society, pp. 6 (neg. #63-221.18), 20–21 (neg. #63-221.45), 53 (bottom), 58 (neg. #696), 73 (neg. #63-221.65); Russell Lamb Photography, p. 70; Montana Historical Society, Helena, pp. 63, 65; National Museum of American Art, Washington, D.C./Art Resource, NY, p. 24; Nez Perce National Historical Park Collection, pp. 27, 49, 50 (left and right), 51 (top and bottom), 52, 53 (top), 54 (top and bottom), 55; Ohio Historical Society, p. 56; Oregon Historical Society, p. 44 (neg. #OrHi 11275); Royal Ontario Museum, p. 2; Slickpoo Collection, p. 10; National Anthropological Archives, Smithsonian Institution, pp. 18 (neg. #2977), 36 (neg. #2923A), 38 (neg. #2987-B-12), 60 (neg. #2953A); Special Collections Division, University of Washington Libraries, pp. 30 (neg. #3436), 46 (neg. #NA 1294), 67 (neg. #NA 1007); U.S. Army Military History Institute, photo by Jim Enos, p. 74; Washington State Historical Society, Tacoma, Washington, pp. 32–33, 35; Historical Photograph Collections, Washington State University Libraries, p. 42.